GOD IS LOVE

Desmond O'Donnell OMI

God is Love

A simplified and abridged version of
Deus Caritas Est
An encyclical letter from
Pope Benedict XVI

the columba press

First published in 2005 by
the columba press
55A Spruce Avenue, Stillorgan Industrial Park,
Blackrock, Co Dublin

Cover by Bill Bolger
Origination by The Columba Press
Printed in Ireland by ColourBooks Ltd, Dublin

ISBN 1 85607 537 0

Acknowledgements

Qutotations from scripture are in the *New Revised Standard Version*, copyright © 1989 by the Division of Christian Education of the National Council of the Churches of Christ in the United States of America and are used by permission.

Note

The purpose of this unofficial and abridged version of the encyclical is to introduce you to the full text. Having read the abridged version, your interest in some parts of it may lead you to read them in greater detail in the encyclical.

Introduction

1. The words 'God is love, and those who abide in love abide in God and God abides in them' (1 Jn 4:16) express the heart of the Christian faith. They describe God, what it means to be human, and what human destiny is.

The words 'So we have known and believe the love that God has for us' (1 Jn 4:16) express the fundamental decision of every Christian. This is the core of Israel's faith (Deut 6:4-5) and gives it new depth and breadth. Love – not just an ethical choice – is central. Love is no longer a mere command; it is a response to the gift of God's love for us in Christ. Jesus has united love of God and love of neighbour.

Today when the name of God is used to justify hatred and violence, this message is timely and significant. This letter is about the love which God lavishes on us and which we are asked to share with others.

The first part is about God's love and about human love. The second part is about how the Church must exercise that love. I wish to call forth a new energy and commitment in our response to God's love.

PART I

The Unity of Love
in Creation and in Salvation History

A problem of language

2. Today the word 'love' is used and misused in many ways but this letter is based on its use in scripture and Church tradition. We speak about love of country, friends, work, family members, parents and children but the love between man and woman would seem to be the perfect example of love. Are all these forms of love basically one or different realities?

'Eros' and 'Agape' – difference and unity

3. The ancient Greeks used the word *eros* to describe the love between man and woman. It is not used in the New Testament and this is significant. The word *agape* is preferred. This points to a new understanding of Christian love. It has been claimed that the Church with its laws, poisoned the word *eros* which offers the Creator's gift of joy as a certain foretaste of the Divine. Does the Church turn to bitterness the most precious things in life ? Is this true ?

4. The Greeks considered *eros* as a kind of intoxication. They called it a 'divine madness' and said that it was a divine power giving supreme happiness. This gave rise to 'sacred' prostitution and fertility cults in temples.

The misuse of *eros* reduced temple prostitutes to mere things. Without rejecting the word, the Old Testament showed that it needed to be disciplined and purified. Otherwise *eros* is just a fleeting pleasure rather than a foretaste to the happiness for which we all yearn.

5. There is a link between purified mature *eros* and the Divine; love promises infinity, eternity. This goal is not attained

by surrendering to instinct. When eros is purified through the path of renunciation it is healed and restored to its true grandeur.

This is so because the human person is body and soul, flesh and spirit. It is neither the body nor the soul alone that loves. It is only when both are united that love – *eros* – is able to attain its true greatness.

Christianity is criticised for opposition to the body and this tendency did exist in the past. Yet, today, *eros* is often reduced to mere 'sex', a commodity, a thing. This is a debasement of the human body. The body then becomes a mere object, disintegrated from our whole being. Authentic *eros* leads us beyond ourselves and tends to rise 'in ecstasy' towards the Divine.

6. In the Song of Songs – perhaps prepared for a Jewish wedding feast – the Hebrew words *dodim* and *ahaba* are used to describe love. *Dodim* expresses a love that it still insecure, unclear and searching. It is later replaced by *ahaba* which expresses a love that is a real discovery of and care for the other. It seeks the good of the one loved through willing sacrifice of oneself. In the Greek New Testament it is translated as *agape*.

This *agape* love grows towards higher levels and inner purification in two ways. It is exclusive love for one person and it is 'for ever'. This love becomes a journey from inward-looking self to the freedom of self-giving. It leads to true self-discovery and to the discovery of God. Jesus walked this path from self sacrifice to the resurrection. The grain of wheat that falls into the ground and dies bears much fruit. This is the essence of love and indeed of human life itself.

7. We ask now if these different meanings of the word 'love' point to some unity or are they unconnected?

Eros and *agape* are often called love from below and love coming from above – ascending and descending love respectively. However, they can never be completely separated. Even if *eros* is at first possessive, it is accompanied by the need for real happiness in drawing near to the other. It gradually becomes less concerned with itself and seeks to be present for the other. At this moment the element of *agape* is entering into love. If it does not, *eros* remains impoverished. On the other hand, one cannot live *agape* alone. One cannot always give, one must also receive. In order to be a source of love, one must keep in contact with Jesus Christ, from whose pierced heart flows the love of God.

8. We have seen that love is a single reality but with different dimensions. At different times, one or other dimension may emerge more clearly. If they are cut off from each other the result is an impoverishment of love. Biblical faith does not set up a parallel universe. It intervenes in the human search for love in order to purify it and to reveal new dimensions of it. It reveals a new image of God and of the human person.

The newness of biblical faith
9. The Bible revealed a true image of God in the *Shema* – 'Hear, O Israel: The Lord is our God, the Lord alone' (Deut 6:4). All other gods are not God. The whole universe came into being by the power of God's creative Word and his creation is dear to him. His love chose Israel and he loves her with a view to healing the whole human race. God loves, and his love may certainly be called *eros*. Yet it is also totally *agape*.

The prophets, particularly Hosea and Ezekiel, described God's passion for his people in erotic images such as engagement, marriage, adultery and prostitution. God's love for Israel was shown by giving her the Torah. This is the law which opened peoples' eyes to man's deepest nature. It also guided humanity's path to true humanness and happiness.

10. As we saw, God's *eros* for people is also totally *agape*. It was a love given without having been earned. God's passionate love for his people is at the same time a forgiving love after infidelity. He reconciled justice and love in forgiveness. 'My compassion grows warm and tender' (Hos 11:8). This description of God's love prefigures his love in becoming human and in dying on the cross.

God, the absolute and ultimate source of all being, is at the same time a lover with all the passion of true love. In this way *eros* is supremely ennobled. At the same time it is so purified that it becomes one with *agape*. For this reason the human person can indeed enter into union with God – a union towards which he or she deeply aspires. In this union, God and the human person remain themselves, but they become fully one (1 Cor 6:17).

11. Biblical faith gives a new image of God and a new image of the human person. After Adam's creation, even though he had named all the other creatures, he could not find one to help him. Then Eve was created and Adam said, 'This at last is bone of my bones and flesh of my flesh' (Gen 2:23). Alone, Adam was incomplete. With Eve, he became complete. The idea is certainly present that man is somehow incomplete, driven by nature to seek another who can make him whole, and that only in communion with the other sex can one become complete.

Thus *eros* is somehow rooted in man's very nature. Adam is a seeker in order to find woman; only together do the two represent complete humanity and become one flesh. From the standpoint of creation, *eros* directs man towards marriage in a bond which is unique and definitive. Like God's relationship with his people and vice versa, this bond is exclusive and definitive. This link between *eros* and marriage has almost no equivalent outside the Bible.

Jesus Christ – the incarnate love of God

12. The Old and The New Testament blend with each other profoundly. The real novelty of the New Testament is that the thoughts of the Old become flesh very realistically in Christ. In him God himself goes in search of the stray sheep, of a suffering and lost humanity. By his death on the cross, Christ shows us that 'God is love' (1 Jn 4:8) and in this we discover the path along which Christian life and love must move.

13. Jesus gave his offering an enduring presence in the Eucharist – the new manna. The ancient world had dimly perceived that what really nourished the human person was eternal wisdom. In the New Testament this eternal wisdom now becomes eternal love and man's real food. In the Eucharist we

enter into the very dynamic of Christ's self-giving. In the Old Testament the image of marriage between God and the human person meant standing in God's presence. In the New Testament it becomes a union with God's gaciously condescending love through sharing in Christ's body and blood.

14. This union with Christ is also union with all those to whom he gives himself. 'Because there is one bread, we who are many are one body, for we all partake of the one bread' (1 Cor 10:17). I cannot possess Christ just for myself. I can belong to him only in union with all those who have become, or will become his own. Love of God and love of neighbour are now truly united: God incarnate draws us all to himself. Love of others is no longer simply a matter of morality, of obedience to laws alongside faith in Christ. Worship and ethics unite. Eucharist communion includes the reality of being loved and of loving others in turn. A celebration of the Eucharist which does not pass over into a concrete practice of love is essentially fragmented.

15. The parables of the rich man who neglected the poor man (Lk 16:19-31) and of the Good Samaritan who loved an enemy (Lk 10:25-37) show us that love cannot be confined to family, friends or fellow citizens. The idea of 'neighbour' is now universalised. But it must also be concrete, calling for personal practical commitment here and now. In the parable of the Last Judgement,(Mt 25:31-46), Jesus identifies himself with everyone in need. In the least of our brothers and sisters we find Jesus himself, and in Jesus we find God.

Love of God and love of neighbour
16. Can we love God without seeing him? In his first letter, St John tells us that love of others is a path that leads to the encounter with God. 'Those who say, "I love God" and hate their brothers and sisters, are liars; for those who do not love a brother or sister whom whom they seen, cannot love God whom they not seen' (1 Jn 4:20). Closing our eyes to our neighbour also blinds us to God.

17. God has made himself visible in Jesus. 'Whoever has seen

me has seen the Father' (Jn 14:9). By his life he seeks to win our hearts all the way to the Last Supper, to the piercing of his heart on the cross, to his appearance after the resurrection and in the early Church. We can meet him in men and women who reflect his presence. We also meet him in the Church's liturgy.

Feelings come and go, but love is not merely a feeling. Yet, a feeling can be a first spark. Mature love then deepens to engage the whole person. It is in contact with visible manifestations of God's love that we experience being loved. And each time I say 'yes' to God's will I grow in his love. When I accept that God is more present to me than I am to myself, self-abandonment to God increases, and God becomes my joy (Ps 73:23-28).

18. In God and with God I love even the person whom I do not like or even know. This can take place only when I have an intimate encounter with God in a communion of wills which affects even my feelings. Then I look at the other through the eyes of Jesus Christ. If I fail completely to heed others out of my desire to perform my 'religious duties', then my relationship with God will become arid. Only if I serve my neighbour can I be open to what God does to me, and to how much he loves me. Love of neighbour is no longer a 'commandment' imposed from without. It is a freely bestowed experience of love from within, a love which by its very nature must then be shared with others, until in the end God is 'all in all' (1 Cor 15:28).

PART II

Caritas: The Practice of Love by the Church as a 'Community of Love'

The Church's charitable activity as a manifestation of Trinitarian love
19. 'If you see charity, you see the Trinity' (St Augustine). In the pierced one we recognise the Father's love. By dying on the cross Jesus 'gave up his Spirit' (Jn 19:30) and this enabled him to send the Holy Spirit after his resurrection. The Holy Spirit harmonises our hearts with the heart of Christ. It then moves us to love others, like Christ who washed the feet of his disciples (Jn 13:1-13) and gave his life for us.

The Spirit also transforms the heart of the Church community so that it can become a witness before the world of the Father's love. The entire activity of the Church is an expression of this love which seeks the full welfare of each human person. It seeks each one's evangelisation through word and sacrament and it seeks to promote all human life and activities. Love is the service of the Church which cares for human suffering and human needs, including material needs. I wish to speak about this now.

Charity as a responsibility of the Church
20. Individually every Christian must practise love. It is also the responsibility of the entire Church community locally and universally. As a community, the Church must practise love in an organised way. Within the community of believers there can be no room for a poverty that denies anyone what is needed for a dignified life.

21. In the early Church the Apostles felt the need to concentrate primarily on 'prayer and on the ministry of the word' (Acts 6:1-6). So they chose seven others to perform social service to the community. This service was also a spiritual service through an

absolutely concrete love of neighbour. This orderly exercise of charity to the community is part of the fundamental structure of the Church.

22. The Church cannot neglect the exercise of charity any more than she can neglect the sacraments and the word. Justin Martyr, who died around 155 AD, mentions charitable activity linked with the Eucharist. About the year 200 Tertullian related how the pagans were struck by the Christians' concern for the needy of every sort.

23. The development of this service *(diakonia)* became a structured activity in the Church, especially in Egypt and in Rome. When St Lawrence was ordered by civil authorities to give the treasures of the Church to the authorities, he sold them and he gave the funds to the poor. He then presented the poor to the authorities as the real treasures of the Church.

24. The emperor Julian the Apostate, who died in 363, tried to supplant the Church as the centre of peoples' lives. He said that the Church's charitable activity was the reason for the popularity of the 'Galileans' and so he set up an equivalent system of organised charity for his pagan religion. In doing this he confirmed that charity was a decisive feature of the Christian community.

25. The Church's deepest nature is expressed in her threefold responsibility of proclaiming the word of God (*kerygma*), of celebrating the sacraments (*leitourgia*) and of exercising the ministry of charity (*diakonia*). These presuppose each other and are inseparable. For the Church, charity is not a kind of welfare activity which could be equally well left to others, but it is an indispensable expression of her very being.

No one in the Church should have to go without the necessities of life, but *Caritas-agape* extends beyond the frontiers of the Church. The parable of the Good Samaritan is the standard which imposes universal love towards the needy everywhere. As St Paul wrote, 'So then, whenever we have an opportunity, let work for the good of all, and especially to those of the family of faith' (Gal 6:10).

Justice and Charity

26. Works of charity can be a way for the rich to shirk their obligation to work for justice. They can preserve their own status while robbing the poor of their rights. The pursuit of justice must be a fundamental norm of the State, assuring that each person receives his share of the community's goods. The rise of modern industry caused old social structures to collapse. The relationship between capital and labour became the decisive issue. Money and the means of production became the new source of power concentrated in the hands of a few. The rights of the poor were suppressed and so they rebelled.

27. Apart from a few pioneers, the Church's leadership was slow to recognise that the just structuring of society needed to be approached in a new way. In 1891 Pope Leo XIII intervened with an important letter, as did other Popes up until Pope John Paul II who wrote three letters on social justice. The Church's present guidelines must be used in dialogue with all those who are seriously concerned for humanity and for the world in which we live.

28. To define more accurately the relationship between commitment to justice and the ministry of charity, two situations need to be considered.

a) The just ordering of society and the State is a central responsibility of politics. 'A State which is not governed according to justice would be a bunch of thieves' (St Augustine). The State may not impose religion yet it must guarantee religious freedom and harmony between followers of different religions. Church and State are distinct yet always interrelated.

The State must aim to achieve justice through the use of practical reason. But reason must be constantly purified lest power and special interests lead to ethical blindness.

Here politics and faith meet, because faith liberates reason from its blind spots and helps it to do its work more effectively. Catholic social doctrine has no intention of giving the Church power over the State or trying to impose thought and behaviour on those who do not share the faith. Its sole aim is simply to purify reason and help it attain what is just.

Although the Church's social teaching is built on the nature of every human being, it is not the Church's responsibility to make its teaching prevail in political life. Rather, the Church wishes to help form consciences for political life and to offer her own specific contribution towards the achievement of justice.

The Church cannot and must not replace the State but she must try to bring about openness of mind and will, to the demands of justice and of the common good.

b) Even in the best-ordered State, love (*caritas*) will be necessary. To eliminate love is to eliminate the human. There will always be suffering in need of consolation, loneliness and unsatisfied material needs. Every person needs loving personal concern. Social forces, of which the Church is one, must support charitable initiatives. The Spirit of Christ in the Church enkindles love which provides material help, refreshment and care of people's souls. 'One does not live by bread alone' (Mt 4:4).

29. The formation of just structures belongs to the world of politics, not to the Church. The Church is called to help purify reason through which just structures are formed. She is also called to reawaken the moral forces without which just structures are either not established or not effective.

Lay believers have the duty to work for a just society. They must participate in economic, social, legislative, administrative and cultural areas of society. Charity must animate their entire lives and therefore their political activity also.

By her very nature, the Church has direct responsibility to practise charity as an organised activity. At the same time, the charity of each individual believer is necessary.

The multiple structures of charitable service in the social context of the present day

30. I now wish to describe the overall situation of the struggle for justice and love in the world today.

a) Today the mass media have made our planet smaller. We can know almost instantly about the needs of others, and this challenges us to share their situation and their difficulties.

Despite great scientific advances there is much suffering in the world on account of material and spiritual poverty. Our times call for a new readiness to assist our neighbours in need.

We now have at our disposal many means for offering food, clothing, housing and care to our brothers and sisters in need. State agencies and humanitarian associations work to promote this beyond what individuals alone can accomplish.

b) The co-operation between State and Church has been very successful. Christian agencies are able to give a Christian quality to the civil agencies. Our time has also seen the growth of different kinds of volunteer work, which assumes responsibility for providing a variety of services. I wish to offer gratitude and appreciation to the many volunteers who take part in these activities. This movement gives young people a school of life which offers them formation in solidarity and self-giving. This unselfish love counters the current anti-culture of death, for example in the abuse of drugs.

The distinctiveness of the Church's charitable activity
31. The command to love one's neighbour is inscribed in the human heart. This is why the number of organisations engaged in meeting human needs is increasing. Christianity constantly revives and acts out this human imperative. Nevertheless it is very important that the Church's charitable activity does not become another form of social assistance.

I wish now to outline the distinctive essential elements of Christian and ecclesial charity:

a) Christian charity is first of all the simple response to immediate needs and specific situations. The Catholic organisation *Caritas* ought to do everything in its power to provide the resources and the professionally competent personnel needed for its work. However, individuals need more than technically proper care; they need humanity. They need heartfelt concern enabling them to experience the richness of their humanity. That is why charity workers need a formation of the heart. They need to encounter God in Christ. Then their love will no longer be a commandment but an expression of 'faith working through love' (Gal 5:6).

b) Christian charitable activity is not a means of changing systems of ideas or of helping worldly policies. It is a way of making present the love which the human person always needs. Charity has been rejected by some as slowing down a potential revolution to establish a better world. But one cannot make the world more human by refusing to act humanely here and now. At the same time, charitable activity by the Church must be combined with planning, foresight and co-operation with other institutions.

c) Love is free; it is not practised in order to achieve other ends. Love never seeks to impose the Church's faith upon others. Yet the Christian must not leave God and Christ aside because he or she must be concerned about the spiritual welfare of the whole person. The deepest cause of suffering is often the very absence of God. A Christian knows when it is time to speak of God and when it is better to say nothing and to let love alone speak. We know that God's presence is felt, even when the only thing to do is to love.

Those responsible for the Church's charitable activity

32. Bishops have the primary responsibility for making sure that the Church is a place where help is given and received. At his ordination, the bishop promises to be welcoming and merciful to the poor. The recent Directory for the Pastoral Ministry of Bishops emphasises that the exercise of charity is an essential part of the Church's mission.

33. The persons who carry out the Church's charitable activity must be persons whose hearts are conquered by Christ's love. 'For the love of Christ urges us on' (2 Cor 5:14). In Christ, God has given himself to us unto death. This must inspire them to live no longer for themselves but for him and with him for others. By sharing in the Church's practice of love, they wish to be witnesses of God and of Christ and for this reason do good freely for all.

34. Charity workers do work in harmony with other organisations but in a way which respects what is distinct about Christian discipleship. The hymn to charity (1 Cor 13) teaches us that real charity is more than activity alone. It is always motivated by love. 'If I give away all I have, and if I deliver my body to be burned, but do not have love, I gain nothing; (v 3). My personal sharing in the needs and sufferings of others becomes a sharing of my very self with them. I must be personally present in my gift.

35. One must not consider oneself superior to the one served. In helping others we must realise that in doing so we receive help. The duty we perform is a grace because the Lord has enabled us to do so. We are only instruments in the Lord's hands. In all humility we will do what we can with the strength we have, and entrust the rest to the Lord.

36. When we consider the immensity of others' needs we might feel driven to resolve every problem or tempted to give in to doing nothing. At times like this, a living relationship with Christ is decisive, and prayer is the means of drawing ever new strength from Christ.

37. Many Christians give in to activism or secularism by neglecting prayer. In prayer the Christian asks God to be present with the consolation of the Spirit. An authentically religious attitude also prevents us from presuming to judge God, accusing him of allowing poverty, and failing to have compassion for his creatures.

38. Often we cannot understand why God refrains from intervening in the presence of deprivation or suffering. But, as St Augustine tells us, if we were able to understand God, God would not be God. God does not prevent us from crying out 'My God, my God, why have you forsaken me ?' (Mt 27:46). Our crying out, similar to Jesus on the cross, is the deepest and most radical way of affirming our faith in his sovereign power. Even in their bewilderment and failure to understand the world around them, Christians continued to believe in 'the goodness and loving kindness of God' (Tit 3:4). We remain certain of his love even when his silence remains incomprehensible.

39. Faith, hope and charity go together. Hope is practised through patience and humility. We accept God's mystery and trust him even at times of darkness. Faith gives us the victorious certainty that God has given his Son for our sake. Love transforms our doubts into the sure hope that God holds the world in his hands and that he will ultimately triumph. Faith also sees God's love in Christ's pierced heart, and gives rise to love. Love is the light – and in the end, the only light –that can always illuminate a world grown dim, and give us the courage needed to keep living and working. Love is possible, and we are able to practise it because we are created in the image of God. To experience love and in this way to cause the light of God to enter into the world – this is the invitation I would like to extend with the present letter.

Conclusion

40. St Martin of Tours gave half his cloak to a poor man and that night Jesus appeared to him in a dream wearing that cloak. After meeting God intimately, St Anthony the Abbot made hospitality, refuge and care of the infirm central to the monastic vocation. Many founders of religious institutes did the same.

41. Mary, the mother of the Lord, put God at the centre of her life – 'My soul glorifies the Lord.' She does not put herself at the centre but leaves space for God whom she encounters both in prayer and in service of her neighbour. She knows that she will contribute to the salvation of the world if she places herself completely at God's disposal. She is a woman of hope because she believes God's promises and accepts her call to serve these promises. Mary is the woman of faith – 'Blessed are you who believed' (Lk 1:45). She is the woman of the Word because she speaks and thinks with the Word of God; the Word of God becomes her word. Mary is the woman who loves. We find her engaged in serving her cousin Elizabeth (Lk1:56), and we see the delicacy with which she recognises the need of the spouses at Cana (Jn 2). She recedes into the background during Jesus' public life knowing that her Son must establish a new family. She remains beneath the cross when the disciples flee, and the disciples gather around her as they await the Holy Spirit at Pentecost (Acts 1:14).

42. The saints who draw near to God do not withdraw from fellow humans but become truly close to them. Jesus' words to John – 'Behold your mother' – are fulfilled in every generation. Mary has truly become the mother of all believers who have constant recourse to her kindness in their joys and sorrows. The

goodness and unfailing love which she pours out from the depths of her heart, comes from her most intimate union with God. Mary, Virgin and Mother, shows us what love is, and from where its constantly renewed power comes. To her we entrust the Church and its mission in the service of love:

Holy Mary, Mother of God,
you have given the world its true light,
Jesus, your Son – the Son of God.
You abandoned yourself completely
to God's call
and thus became a wellspring
of the goodness which flows forth from him.
Show us Jesus. Lead us to him.
Teach us to know and love him,
so that we too can become
capable of true love
and be fountains of living water
in the midst of a thirsting world.

The Pope issued the Encyclical on 25 December 2005.

Questions for Reflection

1. Why do these words, 'God is love, and he who abides in love abides in God and God abides in him' (1 Jn 4:16) express the heart of the Christian faith? (Introduction)

2. In what way do the words, 'We have come to know and to believe in the love God has for us' (1 Jn 4:16) express a decision in your life? (Par 1)

3. Is *eros*, which means passionate love, an end in itself or how do you think it could lead to something richer? (Par 5)

4. Have you ever suspected that Christian teaching in the past has tended towards a negative view of our bodies, and why? (Par 5)

5. How do you react to the eroticism, the sensuality, of The Song of Songs? (Par 6)

6. In what way do the Hebrew words *dodim* and *ahaba* differ in meaning? (Par 6)

7. Why can God's love be described as erotic – *eros*? (Par 9)

8. What is your own description of the word *agape*? (Par 10)

9. Why is Jesus the a very realistic expression of God's *agape* for us? (Par 12)

10. Why is the exercise of *agape* more a source of energy and a privilege, than an obligation ? (Pars 14, 18 & 31a)

11. Even after performing your 'religious' duties, how could your relationship with God become arid? (Par 18)

12. What is the difference in the same social work being carried out by a believer and a non-believer? (Par 34)

13. Why is it important that the Church's charitable activity does not become merely another form of social assistance? (Pars 31 & 31b)

14. Why will charity always be necessary even in a well-ordered society? (Par 28b)

15. In the past, Church leadership was slow to realise that the just structuring of society needed a new approach. Could you also be slow to realise that some people in your area may not have all the necessities for a dignified life? (Pars 20 & 27)

16. How did Mary put God's *agape* at the centre of her heart and at the centre of her actions? (Par 41)

17. How do you respond to God's apparent failure to prevent unexplained suffering, earthquakes and tsunamis? (Par 38)

18. In what way might the Good Samaritan's hospitality to a stranger, and the rich man's failure to share, apply to Irish Christians today? (Par 15)

19. How could Mass-going be accompanied by an essentially fragmented Christian life? (Pars 13 & 14)

20. What difference do you think this encyclical will make to your life ?